Literally
Short &
Sweet

Jeanie Buckingham

Dedicated to my Auntie Eileen, born and bred in Bishops Tachbrook, who gave me a Parker pen and a bottle of Quink Ink for my 11th birthday on 1st September 1956, ready for me to take to my new school two days later. Having left the village school that day, where Auntie Eileen had also spent her school days, from a class of fourteen pupils in Tachbrook, I found in Leamington I was in a class of forty-eight and was one of the youngest in the class. At a Leamington Spa Comprehensive School where I spent four tortured years, I sat next to Linda, who was twelve months older than me, all but eight days, her birthday being on 9th September 1944. I am still in touch with her.

CONTENTS

6

CLERIHEWS

(If you don't know what a clerihew is, this is your chance to find out.)

If you haven't got anything else to do

Then you can write a Clerihew

Four lines which needn't scan; the rhymes are few

To be precise there are only two.

Exactly, this is not a Clerihew.

Edmund Clerihew Bentley

invented magnificently,

a name, four lines, two rhymes, a witty verse,

descriptive, biographical, terse.

Gerard Manley Hopkins

Essex lad, turned Jesuit, so may have worn stockings,

sprung like a goat, nimbly skipping along the lines of his verse;

some people liked it, and let's be honest it could have been worse.

Emily Bronte

in a Yorkshire parsonage sat and sipped tea,

wrote with her two sisters, alongside each other; pen in hand, poetry, a novel, she wrote about love, usually doomed and the lie of the land.

Andrew Marvell

knew a coy mistress who was cold as marble.

Andy felt time was running out and tried very hard to persuade her of the joys of taking a mate.

I'm sure it's something we've all thought – if you don't get a move on, it'll be too late.

Edgar Allan Poe

The Raven, not the crow,

at forty, his death, as macabre and mysterious, as his writing,

all his unhappy life an alcohol addicted victim, he was never likely to go out courageously fighting.

Robert Herrick

A seventeenth century cleric

liked women's clothing, admired the rippling movement

but on further reflection he decided he preferred their removement.

Branwell

the ne'er do well,

scoundrel brother of the Bronte sisters, that famous threesome, they lived in fear,

of what he would do next, but, as he wasn't a poet, he really shouldn't be here

Anon

is some mother's daughter or some mother's son

but they never seem to want to take the credit

even though we've loved it when we've read it.

Hilaire Belloc

promoted havoc

with rhymed nursery tales of frightful children

at the end of which bizarre circumstances usually killed 'em.

Robert Frost

Indecisive when lost,

he often stood still looking, admiring the view, which way to go was the question,

always carry a flask of tea to drink, while you think, is my suggestion.

Thomas Hardy

lived in Dorset, and was sometimes mardy,

he had a wife, who he didn't much like, until she died,

and then poor Thomas, he cried and cried.

William Blake

for goodness sake:

Little lamb who made thee?

Let's look in the yellow pages under lamb-makers shall we?

Alexander Pope

liked a joke,

mostly satirical, observational ridicule, a well-aimed dart;

but poor Alex was not very lucky in affairs of the heart.

Percy Bysshe Shelley

poet, dashing young lover, should have taken the ferry.

I'm not sure whether he was swimming or boating, the silly fool, anyway he ended up floating; it put a damper on the afternoon.

William McGonagall

poetic paragon,

his Taybridge Disaster was hilariously funny.

I hope he made a lot of money.

Ted Hughes

I have to accuse

of being born in Yorkshire and not playing cricket,

he was married to Sylvia but just couldn't stick it.

Dylan Thomas

too soon was taken from us.

Welsh playboy and poet, he lived in Laugharne, next to the river,

but at the age of thirty-nine the alcohol 'did for' his liver.

W H Auden

wrote to Lord Byron but not General Gordon;

in '39 he sailed with Chris Ish, up, off and away,

draft dodging, then nationalising himself in the U.S. of A.

Edith Sitwell

I'm sorry to say didn't fit well

into everyday life, good thing then she was upper middle-class; the poetic eccentric

who thought she was Elizabeth the First. Very acerbic.

George Gordon, Lord Byron

was a bit of a wry one,

much like myself, wrote epics, lived in an abbey, fought against Turkey,

unlike myself he lived a life that was rather murky.

Ezra Pound

In my book is not to be found,

so, I don't know if he shopped at Primark or Poundland,

but, I really hope he came from Newfoundland.

Alfred Tennyson, Lord

please stand and applaud,

he wrote about six hundred men charging, Maud, and the garden gate.

We know only a handful of charging men survived, but Maud and the gate: we don't know their fate.

Michael Rosen

has been chosen

to be the Children's Poet Laureate – clever dick,

I expect that made the others sick.

John Clare

made everyone aware

that you don't always need schooling to be a poet.

The problem for the intelligent, but poor, is they don't
always have a way to show it.

Christina Rossetti

her last name rhymes with spaghetti.

Christina wrote poems about goblins, markets, and berries,

and a bleak, cold midwinter, when you needed a warm coat
and wellies

John Donne

was a lot of fun,

or at least he sounds it in his writing,

but when he found religion he became a lot less exciting.

Carol Ann Duffy

is not at all fluffy,

she's our Poet Laureate, but please don't call her Pee Ell,

very strangely she's a poet whose books actually sell.

Carol Ann Duffy

is not at all fluffy,

T S Eliot

a poet of merit,

to his credit, he gave us the OC, and told us how to name the cat.

I would have given him, The Apricot and the Peaches, I wonder what he would have made of that.

she's our Poet Laureate, but please don't call her Pee Ell,

John Betjeman

a prolific poetic battering ram;

he wrote about a death in Leamington in verse,

not his death, of course, so it could have been worse.

very strangely she's a poet whose books actually sell.

Andrew Motion

expressed devotion

to his Mum's old Aga,

he put it in a poem but it's not a saga.

very strangely she's a poet whose books actually sell.

Philip Larkin

tough as shark skin.

Poet, librarian, in his writing

very biting.

very strangely she's a poet whose books actually sell.

Stevie Smith

remained a poetic 'myth'.

Florence Margaret, known as Stevie, never wed.

She had a hot-water bottle to keep her warm in bed.

John Keats

a Romantic poet, wrote sheets and sheets.

A sad short life, despite his love of Fanny,

he didn't ever marry but still he was unhappy.

Wendy Cope

never has to struggle or grope

to find the right words, the ones she chooses

in her humorous poetry, they always amuses.

W B Yeats

is thought of as one of the greats,

he wrote about an old Irish mother,

not his, so it must have been another.

William Shakespeare

let me make it clear

was born in Stratford, then went to London, where he wrote both poetry and plays.

It wasn't Bacon, no matter what anyone says.

Tony Harrison

well, there is no comparison,

we all know that he wrote v well;

what we don't know is do his socks smell?

Geoffrey Chaucer

was the author

of a set of medieval rhymes,

this was a book full of pilgrims, lusty passion, and despicable crimes.

Emily Dickinson

was a US citizen,

a solitary domestic life, her inspiration is not apparent,

she sprinkled dashed commas throughout her hidden talent.

Robert Burns

field mice and lassies took it in turns

to listen to his seductive tartan banter.

He wrote a long poem about a Scot named Tam O'Shanter.

Leigh Hunt

was rather blunt,

he wrote poetry himself, consider Abou Ben Adhem, who
loved his fellow man, but Leigh was highly critical of others,

it didn't make him popular; poets are not always a happy
band of brothers.

Edward Lear

had a successful career.

Limericks sometimes, but also famously of runaway lovers,
a young male owl and a beautiful female pussy-cat, who
with money, and honey, took off into the night, beneath the
stars with the owl playing a guitar and singing, the two of
them sailing in a pea-green boat.

Silly stuff really, but he did compose and draw as well so he
could do more than most.

Dante Alighieri

always wary

of the pitfalls, tipping us into hell; where he made it plain,
we really don't want to be.

A warning lesson for us all, especially me.

Ogden Nash

not Gordon Flash,

you have to smile, laugh out loud at most of it, written very
drily.

Gordon Flash wrote something else entirely.

Sir Philip Sidney

a Renaissance poet of rare ilk and kidney.

He famously wrote a sonnet sequence; it was a lover's plea,
a praising hymn, to a woman he had heartlessly jilted, and
now, of course, realising his mistake repented. But this
former heart throb,

unfortunately for Phil, had gone and married Bob.

Sylvia Plath

was consumed by wrath,

she just couldn't excuse

the way she was treated by Mr Hughes.

Elizabeth Barratt

wrote with her feet up and ate like a rabbit,

carrots, lettuce and radish, were all she was downing,

until her elopement with the carnivore Browning.

Robert Browning

didn't take it lying downing

when Elizabeth Barratt's dad said, 'No,'

he said, 'Pack your bags Liz, off to Italy we'll go.'

Simon Armitage

a writer from Huddersfield, a northern village,

tries to point us in the right direction; North, to the land of fun, 'it's not that grim,'

excitement, glamour, men who are men, and an angel made of tin.

Geoffrey Hill

it would be nice if he were writing still.

He wasn't from Yorkshire, Wales or Ireland, for which we can only admire him,

a Worcs lad, one of his poems, I don't know which, is liked for its vigorous rhythm.

Sir Walter Raleigh

His name may rhyme with Charlie, Rory or Sally.

A poetry writing sailor, famous for his cloak spreading, and yet

Liz had him locked in the Tower; he should have let her get her feet wet.

Craig Raine

I found a pain.

He wrote a poem seeing things through the eyes of a Martian.

I didn't like it but then I am a harsh 'un.

D H Lawrence

married Frieda and visited Florence.

He was born at Eastwood, near Nottingham.

I remember he wrote a poem about a snake but as for the rest I've forgot 'em.

Seamus Heaney

was rather dreamy

his poetry was wonderful, he was no ignoramus

and Suzy and I we both fell for Seamus.

Roger McGough

he pulled it off,

his poetry made him famous,

in fact, even more famous than Seamus.

Gladys Mary Coles,

writer and teacher, doesn't fall down holes,

and has certainly never fallen behind a radiator,

whereas, one of her pupils has fallen backwards down an escalator.

Edmund Spenser

friend to Sir Walter, he was better than the others, a true pre-eminencer

who wrote a very long allegory featuring a faerie queene and a beast who was blatant; both unbelievable

and quite unreadable.

George Crabbe

made a very successful poetic stab

at warning, in his first book, 'Inebriety' (a tome for the AA?) about the perils of drink.

He was admired by Jane Austen and Lord Byron, both of whom were known to consume enough alcohol, in one evening, to make the Titanic sink.

Walter Savage Landor

spoke and wrote with candour,

he warmed his hands before the fire of life, but when it burned low,

he was ready to go.

William Wordsworth,

Lake District poet, wrote some very fine stuff,

He is reckoned by some

To be England's number one.

Arthur Hugh Cluffe,

of whom, his admiring friends couldn't get enough,

apparently wrote splendid poetry and such,

although, nowadays you don't hear of him much.

Algernon Charles Swinburne,

as a Poet Laureate, he never got a turn.

Wrote short little ditties

about girls who lived in cities.

Charles Lamb

Lived with his sister, Mary Ann,

both of them meek and mild as Larry, though she had once done something that shocked.

He thought he would be alright as long as he kept the knife drawer locked.

Thom Gunn

didn't want to be outdone,

deciding in England his chance of being venerated was slim,

he upped sticks to the U.S. where, fortunately, the Americans adored him.

George Herbert

well born, country rector, wrote a surfeit

of sweet verses, mostly short with ingenious images,
inimitable;

the title of his book reflecting the truly divine and
metaphysical.

Colley Cibber

although A. Pope thought he was fraudulently dull, he was
in fact endlessly jolly, good humoured and chipper.

Deservedly buried in Poets Corner, Westminster Abbey, the
only fitting place for the Poet Laureate,

he may well have been taken to Heaven in a flower-decked
flying chariot.

Walter de la Mare

for children, wrote more than his share;

the three farmers were incredibly jolly

but a lot of the others are rather melancholy.

Samuel Taylor Coleridge

as long as he kept up his opium intake there was no shortage,

his poetic output under the influence was phenomenal.

Would he have done so well if he had been taking paracetamol?

Jonathan Swift

was permanently miffed, but possessed a gift

for describing the foibles, follies and fickleness of the human race,

he was on the side of the poor and oppressed, as long, of course, as they stayed in their place.

William Cowper

often unhappy still he did his best to be a steadfast trooper,

wrote divertingly about John Gilpin, who went on a wild ride on a horse – it wasn't a mare –

he should have got off at Edmonton but it carried him on to Ware.

HAIKU & TANKAS

encapsulating

poetry in a bottle

the haiku genii

counting syllables

seventeen no more no less –

haikus are the dev

just because you can

write seventeen syllables

doesn't mean you should

this syllable count

ing can be rather confus

ing when starting out

LIVERPOOL
HAIKU

Liver Building roof

talisbirds of the city;

sharp-eyed observers.

A landmark beacon

throwing waves and beams across

Liverpool city

Below ground cavern

Beatles sung, under the sea

Yellow Submarine

Footballs, blue and red
Shirts worn by devoted fans
Iconic players

Top of Brownlow Hill
Victoria Gallery's
red brick clock tower

Metropolitan
our iconic cathedral
stone bronze glass glory

Jacob Epstein's bronze
Liverpool Resurgence; known
as Dickie Lewis.

The Hall of St George

has stone lions at the front,

a garden at the rear.

Queen Victoria,

an example of female/

male equality

Ancient school building,

a creative meeting place,

art and poetry.

Fused yellow hybrid,

its off-spring coloured, patterned,

stand round the city.

A dome, central stairs,

magical architecture,

books held up by air.

Toad-like appearance

squat, crouch'd, ugly, brown; innards

a vast open space.

An enormous wheel

from which to view sea, sky, land;

revolving eye pods.

Tate, sugar magnate,

renovated dock warehouse

modern art displays.

Docks, trunks, cargo, ships,

cabins, holds, passengers, crew;

departure city.

Thoroughbred horses

chosen for speed, pass the post

with flying colours.

Beneath the water,

excavational diggers,

gave transport access.

World; Liverpool Life;

rooms, displays, exhibits, each

telling a story.

Brass and glass tap rooms,

photographs of ships adorn

ceramic tiled walls.

Crossing the Mersey

river boat once rowed by monks

now engine powered.

Music hall, concerts,

between the two cathedrals

harmony stretches.

Adelphi, the third.

Palatial hotel, welcomes

tourists on coach tours.

Brick built, water-side,

six clocks, alarm bell, sailors

help, time and warning

Mayor Walker bestowed

a grand building for housing

fine art collections.

Joe Williamson

commissioned tunnels dug, to

benefit the poor.

Oriental arch,

independent state, China,

tea drinker's delight.

Pier Head, old, down at,

the beds were overcrowded.

Move over sailor.

A gentlemen's club,

merchant and professional,

cash talked then, as now.

War damaged St Luke's,

exterior walls still stand

but inside destroyed.

A

CHRISTMAS CAROL

Starting with Marley

Dickens classic – prediction

A warning to Scrooge

A trio of Santas

Make a Christmas Eve visit

Unwelcome at first

Change your behaviour

Your past has been very bad

Repent while there's time

Scrooge changes his ways

Pays out for a big dinner

Tiny Tim is saved

A happy ending

Well maybe but remember

Marley's still in chains

LEAMINGTON
TRAGEDY

Leamington winter

Mother, aunt, daughters set out

Only two return

Sisters holding hands

Victorian tragedy

River ice skating

Breaking ice – bodies

Plucking them from the water

Hooked poles under clothes

Pulled to the bank-side

Carried to a public morgue

Inquest the next day

Accidental death

Future recommendations

Too late – two sisters

WINTER

dashing off haikus

by a bright mid-winter's moon

counting all the way

                        lost lives at Christmas

                how many times have they been warned

                        presents unopened

next year's diary

birthdays filled – death dates unknown

lifeless pages wait

                        night – fairly frosty

                the cavalier king's frost fairs

                        frost moon remembers

in-door cut flowers

placed by the window – reflect

winter sun's low rays

                    standing in a field

           all covered in snow – transformed

               snowmen once scarecrows

dropping from the sky

ten thousand silently swarm

stinging ears and face

swirling in the frosty air

I taste on my tongue – white bees

roofless bombed St Luke's

snow drops – far gentler than bombs

grace healing damage

                                        glass fragment dangles

                                        an unsustainable weight

                                        shards beneath reflect

nativity scene

lanterns coloured balls tinsel

lighting up solstice

year about to be reborn

the sun returning to us

walking past closed doors

a narrow long corridor

would you turn around

                              iced water lilies

                    trapped beneath a hard surface

                        await thaw's hammer

brake lights – hazards

shining through the dark night's gloom

rooftop parking space

hooves stamped shaken bells a snort

you won't ever be believed

feet making arrows

direction you have travelled

through time and new snow

                  threadbare appearance

          patches tatters – once smooth green

              tufts showing through snow

rose endures winter

love's bloom, blood-red petals shed

the sharp thorns remain

               from the north – wind blows

                facing head on my future

                  I turn – watch you go

SPRING

garden pond frozen

heavy sky still air no birds

Jack Frost on the lawn

silence – cold shoulders

frosty looks turned backs ice cold

time passes – we thaw

season with a hint

water wind flower leaf nest

throw in a heron

pioneer settlers

white snowflakes falling outside

claiming the green land

frosty earth – snowflakes

seeking comfort – put down roots

white snowdrops flower

filled buckets of snow

flakes magically transformed

-    to pails of water

one little feather

flies high when carried on the

back of an eagle

piping hot haggis

musical sheep stomach bag

addressed as a guest

an apparition

past occupant glides downstairs

escalating time

St Valentine's Day

verses for the miscreant

invisible ink

messenger service

pushed under door – love letters

I wanted flowers

false declaration

poetry lover who can't

feather down spreading

nestlings shelter beneath mum

wings not yet ready

                                        scoffers debating

                                the price of chocolate eggs

                                            it's all packaging

the cat's at the door

she's wanting to go outside

although it's raining

she insists against advice

returns fur-soaked and angry

SUMMER

the rain turns yellow

when it drops on gold petals

molten gold trickles

flower chains, stalk linked

meadow daisy necklaces

woven by small hands

light-weight, helium

insubstantiality

thistle-down lover

queenly demeanour

we dote, she condescends

graces with a look

fishermen's tackle

lines – maggots in an old tin

bait – patience required

bruised and bleeding knees

medical experts needed –

hugs and chocolate

woodland track – tree roots

earth veins tracking across ground

stop me in my tracks

weaving threading words

links ideas – my mind to yours

carried through the air

read between the lines

an inanimate object

scratches the surface

                                        circus caravans

                              touring performers – nomads

                                        canvas theatre

overcrowded train

sardines in a moving can

bodies breathing in

eyes averted - oily skin –

praying our mobiles don't ring

a mermaid on rocks

beckoning poor doomed sailors

the cake calls to me

                                        magnetic fishing

                        glass bowls cast lines dipped rods

                                    seductively hooked

bird feathers – long pins

a head-dress in which to shop

fashionable hat

fascinating – exotic

flown away with time like you

black amongst the gold

noisy raucous voice – ears ring

crow in a cornfield

                driftwood on tide

         salvaged timbers carried home

              carpenters' harvest

standing on one leg

shrimping pink diet reflects

you are what you eat

              silent as the night

     swans – boring birds world dullards

           no conversation

barn chick-a-biddies

hens grieving for stolen eggs

maternal mourning

empty nest syndrome

does not apply to cuckoos

parental nightmares

sea misadventures

offshore bad behaviour

salt spraying sailors

playing poker, cards

King of Hearts takes Queen of Spades

bluff, win, cut, run, played

kaleidoscope tube

sun dappling through tree tunnel

mosaic pattern

                                        dandelion heads

                            here one minute gone the next

                                        you blew me away

night fox scavenger

noisily invades my dreams

as bins rock and roll

AUTUMN

enthusiastic

strong winds rounding like sheep dogs

leaves into penned piles

                              sycamore seeds twirl

                    seeking fertile ground wind-blown

                              dizzy joyriders

trees keen – nature mourns

leaf loss – bleakness prevails

sleep – survive – resurge

dandelion Heads

here today, gone tomorrow

you blew me away

climbing a mountain

as you're nearing the summit

footholds get scarcer

short memory span

both going round in circles

me and the goldfish

harvest home – corn sheaves

gathered in, church to give thanks

fields full of stubble

clarification

let me be clear fake friend

this lady has turned

staunch church supporters

holy angels feathered wings

flying buttresses

                                        memorial stone

                                a clock in a looking glass

                                    reflecting passed time

bare trees, tomb stones, fog,

a long dead love forgiven

haunted forever

                                        dearly departed

                                for you easier than me

                                    graveyard fugitive

church and cathedral

water drains – pipes gutters spouts

guarded by gargoyles

                    wind ripping through trees

                    you stand with your back turned

                    me blowing kisses

inconsequential

of no or little matter

blown in by the wind

                    graveyard bad weather

                    squelching mud treading water

                    Holy Souls – wet feet

sheep – barb coated fleece

wire wool on knitting needles

sandpaper sweaters

tree fellers felling

pine Christmas trees – forest pines

at their departure

fir trees for Christmas

monkey puzzle is puzzled

why them and not me

curious clusters

cloaked creature contentedly

hanging upside-down

attic nurseries

unassisted toys moving

childhood horror genre

                              he is more worried

                         terrified by the word femme

                            than the word fatale

a noisy arrow

geese - sight and sound instruction

formation flying

                              swinging netted nuts

                     squirrel thief; dextrous movement

                                    ingenuity

driving through the mist

moorland cattle watch closely

threatening headlamps

next door's lawnmower

reminder of Summer days

heard in December

hand-holding lovers

thinking they'll stroll forever

while time is running

still subtle heron

delicate – water colours

willow tree – fish pond

stark statues – stone cold

worthies – Held in high esteem

now frozen in time

winter frost and snow

blind-sided; tactical trick

dying in Autumn

vision essential

low Autumn sun daze, too late

departing footsteps

you wave in the wind

I see you still visible

on the horizon

beech last to unleaf

most unwilling to let go

similar to me

OTHER

cruel people paint

the false self-image we wear

destructive artists

paint stripper needed

peeling away fake layers

detail revealing

restoration work

reclaiming identity

clearly seeing – me

my assets are good

as cool as the next woman's

when they're not frozen

snakes went on the run

when Paddy threatened to put

his boot up their bum

his saintly steel toecaps poised

they all took fright and legged it

                              amateur snappers

                              repositioning nippers

                              unsubtle snippers

Sarcophagi lie

Bandaged well preserved mummies

Torchlight scans the room

Twenty pairs of eyes look back

A night attendant's nightmare

                              Diabetes Ones

                              despise Diabetes Twos

                              'Don't lump us with them'

LIFE AND DEATH

the path is shorter

uphill – difficult walking

approaching the end

turning in the wind

changing your surface colour

reversible coat

dearly departed

for you easier than me

graveyard fugitive

memorial stone

a clock in a looking glass

reflecting passed time

Elysian Fields

an idyllic existence

the end of the Earth

FIVE GRAVE HAIKU

explorers in life

buried now beneath the tree

bravely branching out

no stone is needed

two thousand others, so what

I know where you are

upright once, now bent

natural subsidence or

pushed by those below

ethereal stone

heavenly host, winged herald

bugle flourishes

bare trees, tomb stones, fog

a long dead love forgiven

haunted forever

LITERARY LIMERICKS

(I wrote 44 literary clerihews. I had intended to write
another 44 literary limericks but I only managed 8.)

There once was a young chap, a real toad

who drove fast cars on the open road

Badger, Mole and Ratty

told him he was batty

They were right as a crash later showed

Mary, Kitty, Lydia, Liz, Jane,

one bright, one fancy, two rather plain;

one was a young hussy

and not at all fussy,

running off with a villainous swain.

There once was a lovely fairy queen

who went to sleep in the forest green

along came a yokel

a young Stratford local

a silly ass who still steals the scene.

There was a tiger who came to tea

with all the food he made very free,

all the water he drank,

from both tap and from tank,

then he said, 'Well, it's Goodbye from me.'

Athos, Porthos, and Aramis. Three.

Musketeers. Wearing the Fleur-de-Lis.

Motto; rallying call.

All for one, one for all.

Stars: book, stage, screen and sometimes tv.

Mrs B was sometime unpleasant

when five girls in the house were present

Their dad's vaporous wife,

anguish trouble and strife,

only gin made her effervescent

Jo and her sisters lived with Marmy

Daddy was away in the army

Innocent sweet charming

Aunt March most alarming

Laurie, boy next door, drove them barmy

Fifty Grey Shades a fantasy trip

Women adored an abuser's grip

Feminists were smitten

and longed to be bitten

smacked and tickled by Mr Grey's whip

A nursery rhyme limerick which isn't included in Bim Bam Bong (my children's poetry book)...

In a deep dark wood a bear's house stood

Built on high stilts in case of a flood

Bears go out. House empty.

Bad girl makes her entry.

Bears return; kill girl, eat flesh, drink blood.

ALEXANDER POPE POEMS

Alexander

I admire Mr Pope

who could cut with his pen

right through to the nitty gritty.

I can't do that. I wish I could.

We must face the fact that he was the better writer.

Deciding Factor

There's no-one else I'd sooner be in it with.

Well, Alexander Pope, obviously.

But you have been around for years.

And Alexander rarely puts in an appearance.

Equal to the Task

Alexander Pope would like me.

It's hard not to like someone who likes you.

And I write poetry. A fellow poet.

However, I am not convinced he would read me.

Time Alexander

Both our busy pens stop writing. We look up.

The cat's curled asleep. Midway, gently snoring.

Eyes meet. I know what we are each thinking.

Which one of us will make the tea?

ABOUT THE AUTHOR

Four lines does not always a poet make... but on the Wirral it does. Write at least four and you can't go wrong. Unless you are writing a haiku, in which case any more lines than three will be frowned on. ... The Wirral is top-heavy with male poets but if you have got your hands on this book then you have done well in reversing that trend, as it is written by an old Granny, still living with the cat. This is the fourth book to be written and published by me, as listed here:

Fairly Tall Tales

Cat Chat

Bim Bam Bong

Literally Short and Sweet

Up at Dawn

Up at Dawn

Dressed to kill

Photo shoot

Camera aimed

Professional shot

But it wasn't the

camera or professional

that killed her

It was the shoes

ACKNOWLEDGEMENTS

I am grateful to my daughters, Roanne and Gemma, for all the help they have given me with my books, and in particular to Roanne for the artwork.

I am grateful for the support of my friends, who say kind things about my poetry.

Printed in Dunstable, United Kingdom